Ears

Julie Murray

Peachtree

Abdo
YOUR BODY
Kids

abdopublishing.com

Published by Abdo Kids, a division of ABDO, PO Box 398166, Minneapolis, Minnesota 55439.
Copyright © 2016 by Abdo Consulting Group, Inc. International copyrights reserved in all countries.
No part of this book may be reproduced in any form without written permission from the publisher.

Printed in the United States of America, North Mankato, Minnesota.

102015

012016

THIS BOOK CONTAINS
RECYCLED MATERIALS

Photo Credits: iStock, Shutterstock

Production Contributors: Teddy Borth, Jennie Forsberg, Grace Hansen

Design Contributors: Candice Keimig, Dorothy Toth

Library of Congress Control Number: 2015941990

Cataloging-in-Publication Data

Murray, Julie.
  Ears / Julie Murray.
    p. cm. -- (Your body)
ISBN 978-1-68080-157-6 (lib. bdg.)
Includes index.
1. Ear--Juvenile literature. 2. Hearing--Juvenile literature. I. Title.
612.8/5--dc23
                    2015941990

Table of Contents

Ears

Ears are a part of your body.

Josh touches his ears.

You have two ears. They are on each side of your head.

You use your ears every day.

Anna listens to music.

Ears allow you to hear.

Mark hears his mom talk.

You can hear **soft** sounds.

Grace whispers to her friend.

13

You can hear loud sounds.

The airplane takes off.

Some people can't hear.
They are deaf. They use
sign language.

EAT

DRINK

MORE

PLEASE

THANK YOU

SORRY

17

Animals have ears too.

Elephants have big ears!

What sounds do you hear?

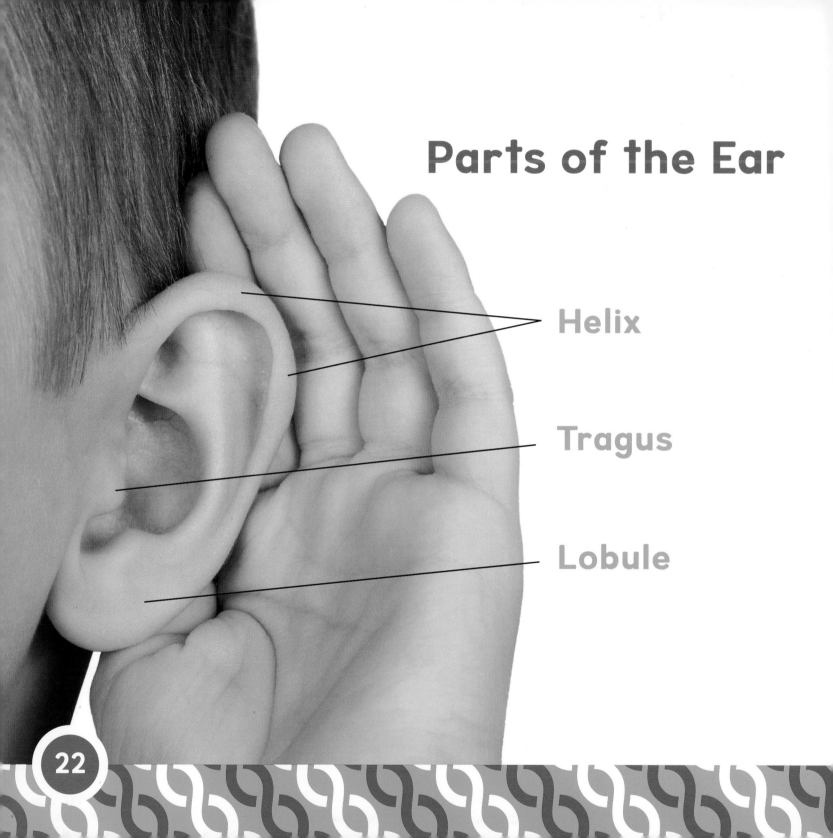

Parts of the Ear

Helix

Tragus

Lobule

Glossary

deaf
partially or fully unable to hear.

sign language
a language that uses hand
movements to communicate.

soft
a way to describe a noise that
is quiet or hard to hear.

Index

abdokids.com

Use this code to log on to abdokids.com and access crafts, games, videos, and more!

Abdo Kids Code:
YEK1576